MW01100696

Activating God's Power

in Michael

by Michelle Leslie

Activating God's Power

DEDICATION

For Michael

Michael,   Feb. 27, 2017
    Just want to wish you a
Happy Birthday! Thought this
could be useful for fun times,
trying times, uncertain times, happy
times, sad times - really ALL times
as it is powerful & truthful!

Blessings,
    Holly

Activating God's Power

CONTENTS

Activating God's Power

Michelle Leslie

ACKNOWLEDGMENTS

Thank you to God, my family, mentors, friends, and neighbors for all your love and support as God prepared me to put this book together.

May the Lord bless you and keep you, the Lord make His face shine upon you and be gracious to you; the Lord turn His face toward you and give you peace.

Numbers 6:24

Activating God's Power

ACTIVATING GOD'S POWER IN YOUR LIFE AND IN OTHERS'

Sometimes we don't know what or how to pray, but we are in need of God's power in our lives. When we pray God's word we can never pray outside God's will for our lives or the lives of others. When we meditate on the word and speak it we are activating God's power. God's word brings life and creates a spiritual mindset that changes us and the world around us (Romans 12:2).

There are many great books on overcoming addiction, having a successful marriage, being effective in ministry, overcoming anxiety, or being a great parent. I challenge you that the solution to all of the above is God's word. There is no formula to solve these issues, but the word of God is alive (Hebrews 4:12) and can empower you to do and be what God is calling you or others to do and be in any circumstance. It transforms the heart and the mind. The word of God brings clarity and strength.

However different from person to person, we all have challenging circumstances and personal weaknesses to overcome. God tells us in the book of Ephesians to use His word (the sword of the Spirit) to fight these battles. We will overcome and will be transformed when we access God's power available in His word. Jesus says in John 8:31-32, "If you abide in my word, you are truly my disciples, and you will know the truth, and the truth will set you free."

God's power is available to each one of us. Activate His power in your life and in the lives of those around you. Speak it, personalize it, and let the power of God transform your life and circumstances.

Anxiety

Michael is strong and courageous. Michael is not afraid or terrified because the Lord his God goes with him; He will never leave him nor forsake Michael."

Deuteronomy 31:6

The Lord goes before Michael and is with him; He will never leave Michael or forsake him. Michael is not afraid or discouraged.

Deuteronomy 31:8

Michael fears no evil because the Lord is with him; God's word and Spirit comfort Michael.

Psalm 23:4

Michael casts his burdens on the Lord, and He sustains him; He will never permit the righteous to be moved.

Psalm 55:22

Anxiety

———— ⟍∽⟍ ————

"Michael comes to me when he labors and is heavy laden, and I give him rest. Michael takes my yoke upon him, and learns from me, for I am gentle and lowly in heart, and he finds rest for his soul. For my yoke is easy, and my burden is light."

Matthew 11:28-30

Peace I leave with Michael; my peace I give to him. Not as the world gives do I give to Michael. Michael lets not his heart be troubled, neither does he lets his heart be afraid.

John 14:27

Michael rejoices in the Lord always and lets his gentleness be evident to all. The Lord is near to Michael so he is not anxious about anything, but in every situation, by prayer and petition, with thanksgiving, he presents his requests to God. And the peace of God, which transcends all understanding, guards Michael's heart and mind in Christ Jesus.

Philippians 4:4-7

Anxiety

Michael casts all his anxiety on Him because He cares for Michael.

1 Peter 5:7

When Michael lies down, he will not be afraid; when Michael lies down, his sleep will be sweet. Michael has no fear of sudden disaster or of the ruin that overtakes the wicked, for the Lord is at his side and will keep his foot from being snared.

Proverbs 3:24-26

Blessing & Favor

May the Lord bless and keep Michael; the Lord make His face to shine on Michael and be gracious to him; the Lord turn His face toward Michael and give him peace.

Numbers 6:24-26

As Michael listens to these commands of the Lord and is careful to obey them, the Lord will make Michael the head and not the tail, and Michael will always be at the top and never at the bottom.

Deuteronomy 28:13

"Oh, that You would bless Michael indeed, and enlarge Michael's territory. May Your hand be with Michael, and keep Michael from evil, that it may not cause him pain.

1 Chronicles 4:10

You gave Michael life and showed him kindness, and in your providence You watch over his spirit.

Job 10:12

Blessing & Favor

May the favor of the Lord our God rest on Michael; and establish the work of Michael's hands—yes, establish the work of Michael's hands.

Psalm 90:17

For You bless the righteous, O Lord; you cover Michael with favor as with a shield.

Psalm 5:12

You prepare a table before Michael in the presence of his enemies; you anoint his head with oil; Michael's cup overflows. Surely goodness and mercy shall follow Michael all the days of his life, and he shall dwell in the house of the Lord forever.

Psalm 23:5-6

Michael is like a tree planted by streams of water that yields its fruit in its season, and its leaf does not wither. In all that Michael does, he prospers.

Psalm 1:3

Blessing & Favor

Michael is blessed because he fears the Lord; he greatly delights in His commandments. Michael's descendants will be mighty on earth; the generation of the upright will be blessed.

Psalm 112:1-2

For the Lord God is Michael's sun and shield; the Lord bestows favor and honor on Michael; no good thing does He withhold from Michael whose walk is blameless.

Psalm 84:11

"Michael's wife shall be like a fruitful vine in the very heart of his house, his children like olive plants (a symbol of anointing) all around his table."

Psalm 128:3

Blessing & Favor

"For I will pour water on Michael when he is thirsty, and floods on the dry ground; I will pour My Spirit on Michael's descendants, and My blessing on Michael's offspring; they will spring up among the grass like willows by the watercourses.

Isaiah 44:3-5

"For I know the plans I have for Michael," declares the Lord, "plans to prosper Michael and not to harm him, plans to give Michael hope and a future."

Jeremiah 29:11

Thank you Lord that it will come to pass that You will pour out Your Spirit on Michael; Michael shall prophesy, dream dreams, and see visions.

Joel 2:28

Blessing & Favor

The heart of Michael is like good soil; he hears the word, accepts it, and produces a crop—some hundred times that which he has sown.

Mark 4:20

He who supplies seed to the sower and bread for food will supply and multiply Michael's seed for sowing and increase the harvest of his righteousness.

2 Corinthians 9:10

Calling

The Lord makes firm the steps of Michael who delights in Him.

Psalm 37:23

Your word is a lamp to Michael's feet and a light to Michael's path.

Psalm 119:105

Michael trusts in the Lord with all of his heart. Michael leans not on his own understanding; in all Michael's ways he acknowledges God and God directs Michael's path.

Proverbs 3:5-6

In his heart Michael plans his course, but the Lord establishes Michael's steps.

Proverbs 16:9

Calling

"For I know the plans I have for you Michael," declares the Lord, "plans for you to prosper and not to harm you, to give you a future and a hope. Then Michael will call upon me and come and pray to me, and I will hear him. Michael will seek me and find me, when Michael seeks me with all of his heart."

Jeremiah 29:11-13

God's gifts and His call on Michael are irrevocable.

Romans 11:29

May the eyes of Michael's heart be enlightened, that he may know what is the hope to which He has called him, what are the riches of His glorious inheritance in the saints.

Ephesians 1:18

Michael lives a life worthy of the calling he has received.

Ephesians 4:1

Calling

He who began a good work in Michael will be faithful to complete it.

Philippians 1:6

For it is God who works in Michael to will and to act in order to fulfill His good purpose.

Philippians 2:13

With this in mind, we constantly pray for Michael, that our God may make Michael worthy of His calling, and that by His power He may bring to fruition Michael's every desire for goodness and deed prompted by faith.

2 Thessalonians 1:11

He has saved Michael and called him to a holy life—not because of anything he has done but because of His own purpose and grace.

2 Timothy 1:9

Calling

When Michael lacks wisdom, he asks God, who gives generously to all without reproach, and it is given to him.

James 1:5

Michael is diligent to confirm his calling and election. As Michael practices these qualities he will never fall.

2 Peter 1:10

Character

Michael's integrity and uprightness protect him, because Michael's hope, Lord, is in you.

Psalm 25:21

Michael does not walk in the counsel of the ungodly or stand in the path of sinners or sit in the seat of scoffers. But Michael delights himself in the law of the Lord and Michael meditates on His law day and night. Michael is like a tree planted by the rivers of water, which yields its fruit in season and whose leaf will not wither, and whatever he does he prospers.

Psalm 1:1-3

Michael walks with integrity; his children are blessed after him.

Proverbs 20:7

Michael is concerned about the Lord's affairs; his aim is to be devoted to the Lord in both body and spirit.

1 Corinthians 7:34

Character

Michael is very careful how he lives—not as unwise but wise, making the most of every opportunity.

Ephesians 5:15-16

God, as one of Your chosen people, holy and dearly loved, help Michael to clothe himself with compassion, kindness, humility, gentleness, and patience.

Colossians 3:12

Michael shows proper respect to everyone. Michael loves the family of believers, fears God, and honors the emperor.

1 Peter 2:17

Direction

Your word is a lamp to Michael's feet and a light to Michael's path.

Psalm 119:105

He refreshes Michael's soul. He guides Michael along the right paths for His name's sake.

Psalm 23:3

"I will instruct Michael and teach him in the way he should go; I will counsel Michael with my eye upon him."

Psalm 32:8

The Lord's angels keep charge over Michael to guard him in all his ways.

Psalm 91:11

The Lord makes firm the steps of Michael, who delights in Him.

Psalm 37:23

Direction

In his heart Michael plans his course, but the Lord establishes Michael's steps.

Proverbs 16:9

Michael trusts in the Lord with all of his heart. Michael leans not on his own understanding; in all Michael's ways he acknowledges God and God directs Michael's path.

Proverbs 3:5-6

The Lord will guide Michael always; He will satisfy Michael's needs in a sun-scorched land and will strengthen Michael's frame. Michael will be like a well-watered garden, like a spring whose waters never fail.

Isaiah 58:11

Discernment

Michael, do not forget my teaching, but let your heart keep my commandments, for length of days and years of life and peace they will add to you. Let not steadfast love and faithfulness forsake you, Michael; bind them around your neck; write them on the tablet of your heart. So you will find favor and good success in the sight of God and man. Trust in the Lord with all of your heart, and do not lean on your own understanding.

Proverbs 3-6:35

Michael does follow the Good Shepherd and Michael knows His voice, and the voice of a stranger Michael will not follow.

John 10:4-5

Michael does not conform to the pattern of this world, but he is transformed by the renewing of his mind. Michael is able to test and approve what God's will is— His good, pleasing and perfect will.

Romans 12:2

Discernment

And this is my prayer: that Michael's love may abound more and more in knowledge and depth of insight, so that Michael may be able to discern what is best and may be pure and blameless for the day of Christ.

Philippians 1:9-10

Michael tests everything. Michael holds on to what is good. Michael avoids every kind of evil.

1 Thessalonians 5:21-22

But solid food is for the mature. By constant use Michael has trained himself to distinguish good from evil.

Hebrews 5:14

Discipline

Michael does not let the book of the Law depart from his mouth. Michael meditates on it day and night. Michael is careful to do everything written in it, so he will be prosperous and successful.

Joshua 1:8

Michael hides God's word in his heart so he is careful to not sin against Him.

Psalm 119:11

Blessed is Michael whom You discipline, O Lord, and You teach Michael out of Your law, to give Michael rest from days of trouble. For the Lord will not forsake Michael; He will not abandon Michael's heritage.

Psalm 94:12-14

Michael does not run aimlessly; he does not fight like a boxer beating the air. But Michael disciplines his body and keeps it under control.

1 Corinthians 9:26-28

Discipline

Michael lives by the Spirit, and does not gratify the desires of sinful nature.

Galatians 5:16

Michael does not let the sun go down on his anger, and he does not give the devil an opportunity.

Ephesians 4:26

Michael does not regard lightly the discipline of the Lord, nor is he weary when reproved by Him. For the Lord disciplines the one He loves, and chastises every child whom He receives.

Hebrews 12:5-6

Encouragement

May the God who gives endurance and encouragement give Michael a spirit of unity with others as he follows Christ Jesus.

Romans 15:5

Michael has encouragement from being united with Christ. Michael has comfort from His love, fellowship with the Spirit, His tenderness and compassion. Michael's joy is complete because he is like-minded with Christ and has the same love and is one with Christ in spirit and purpose. Michael does nothing out of selfish ambition or vain conceit, but in humility, Michael considers others better than himself and looks to the interests of others. Michael's attitude is the same as that of Christ Jesus.

Philippians 2

Encouragement

Michael is encouraged in heart and united in love. Michael has the full riches and complete understanding of the mysteries of God, namely Christ, in whom are hidden all the treasures of wisdom and understanding.

Colossians 2

Faith

Therefore I tell you, whatever Michael asks for in prayer, he believes that he has received it, and it will be his.

Mark 11:24

Faith comes from hearing, and hearing through the word of God. Michael's faith increases every time he hears or reads the word of God.

Romans 10:17

For it is with Michael's heart that he believes and is justified, and it is with his mouth that Michael professes his faith and is saved.

Romans 10:10

Faith

Michael does not lose heart. Though outwardly he is wasting away, yet inwardly Michael is being renewed day by day, for Michael's light and momentary troubles are achieving for him an eternal glory that far outweighs them all. So Michael fixes his eyes not on what is seen, but what is unseen, since what is seen is temporary, but what is unseen is eternal.

2 Corinthians 4:16-18

Michael has been crucified with Christ. Michael no longer lives, but Christ lives in him. The life Michael now lives in the body, he lives by faith in the Son of God, who loved him and gave Himself for him.

Galatians 2:20

Faith

For it is by grace Michael has been saved, through faith—and this is not from yourselves, it is the gift of God—not by works, so that no one can boast. For Michael is God's handiwork, created in Christ Jesus to do good works, which God prepared in advance for Michael to do.

Ephesians 2:8-10

Michael knows that the testing of his faith produces perseverance.

James 1:3

Though Michael has not seen Him, he loves Him; and even though Michael does not see Him now, he believes in Him and is filled with an inexpressible and glorious joy, for Michael is receiving the end result of his faith, the salvation of his soul.

1 Peter 1:8-9

Family

Michael prayed for his child, and the Lord has granted him what he asked of Him.

1 Samuel 1:27

Michael is blessed because he fears the Lord; he delights greatly in His commandments. Michael's descendants will be mighty on earth; the generation of the upright will be blessed.

Psalm 112:1-2

"Michael's wife shall be like a fruitful vine in the very heart of his house, his children like olive plants (a symbol of anointing) all around his table."

Psalm 128:3

Michael walks with integrity; his children are blessed after him.

Proverbs 20:7

Family

Michael has been trained up in the way he should go; and when he is old, he will not depart from it.

Proverbs 22:6

"For I will pour water on Michael when he is thirsty, and floods on the dry ground; I will pour My Spirit on Michael's descendants, and My blessing on Michael's offspring; They will spring up among the grass like willows by the watercourses.

Isaiah 44:3-5

Thus says the Lord: "Michael restrains his voice from weeping, and his eyes from tears; for his work shall be rewarded," says the Lord, "They shall come back from the land of the enemy. There is hope in Michael's future," says the Lord, "That your children shall come back to their own border."

Jeremiah 31:16-17

Family

Michael obeys his parents in the Lord. Michael honors his father and mother so that it may go well with him and that Michael may enjoy long life on earth.

Ephesians 6:1-3

Fear

Michael is strong and courageous. Michael is not afraid or terrified because the Lord his God goes with him; he will never leave him nor forsake Michael.

Deuteronomy 31:6

The Lord goes before Michael and is with him; He will never leave Michael or forsake him. Michael is not afraid or discouraged.

Deuteronomy 31:8

Michael fears no evil because the Lord is with him; God's word and Spirit comfort Michael.

Psalm 23:4

When Michael lies down, he will not be afraid; when Michael lies down, his sleep will be sweet. Michael has no fear of sudden disaster or of the ruin that overtakes the wicked, for the Lord is at his side and will keep his foot from being snared.

Proverbs 3:24-26

Fear

"Michael fears not, I am with him; Michael is not dismayed, for I am his God; I will strengthen Michael, I will help him, I will uphold Michael with my righteous right hand."

Isaiah 41:10

Michael rejoices in the Lord always and lets his gentleness be evident to all. The Lord is near to Michael so he is not anxious about anything, but in every situation, by prayer and petition, with thanksgiving, he presents his requests to God. And the peace of God, which transcends all understanding, guards Michael's heart and mind in Christ Jesus.

Philippians 4:4-7

Michael casts all his anxiety on Him because He cares for Michael.

1 Peter 5:7

Forgiveness

As far as the east is from the west, so far has He removed Michael's transgressions from him.

Psalm 103:12

Michael loves his enemies; he does good to those who hate him.

Luke 6:27

Michael forgives, as the Lord has forgiven him.

Colossians 3:13

"Michael's sins and lawless acts I will remember no more."

Hebrews 10:17

Freedom

Out of Michael's distress he called on the Lord; the Lord answered Michael and set him free.

Psalm 118:5

Michael will know the truth, and the truth will set Michael free.

John 8:32

So if the Son sets Michael free, Michael will be free indeed.

John 8:36

Michael is dead to sin but alive to God in Christ Jesus.

Romans 6:11

Michael has the right to do anything, but not everything is beneficial to him. Michael has the right to do anything, but he will not be mastered by anything.

1 Corinthians 6:12

Freedom

It is for freedom that Christ has set Michael free. Michael stands firm, then, and does not let himself be burdened again by a yoke of slavery.

Galatians 5:1

Michael was called to freedom. Michael does not use his freedom as an opportunity for the flesh, but through love he serves others.

Galatians 5:13

In Him and through faith Michael approaches God with freedom and confidence.

Ephesians 3:12

Michael lives as a person who is free, not using his freedom as a cover-up for evil, but living as a servant of God.

1 Peter 2:16

Grace

God's grace is sufficient for Michael, for His power is made perfect in weakness.

2 Corinthians 12:9

He who began a good work in Michael will be faithful to complete it.

Philippians 1:6

For it is God who works in Michael to will and to act in order to fulfill His good purpose.

Philippians 2:13

Grace and peace be Michael's in abundance through the knowledge of God and of Jesus our Lord. His Divine Power has given Michael everything he needs for a godly life through his knowledge of Him who called Michael by His own glory and goodness.

2 Peter 1:2-3

Healing

Michael serves the Lord his God, and He blesses his bread and his water. He will take sickness away from him.

Exodus 23:25

O Lord my God, Michael cries to You for help, and You have healed him.

Psalm 30:2

Michael blesses the Lord with all his soul, and forgets not all His benefits, who forgives all his iniquity, who heals all his diseases.

Psalm 103:2-3

He sent out His word and healed Michael, and delivered him from his destruction.

Psalm 107:20

Healing

Michael shall not die, but he shall live, and recount the deeds of the Lord.

Psalm 118:17

He heals Michael's broken heart and binds up his wounds.

Psalm 147:3

Michael is not wise in his own eyes; he fears the Lord, and turns away from evil. It is healing to his flesh and refreshment to his bones.

Proverbs 3:7-8

Michael pays attention to what I say; he turns his ear to my words. Michael does not let them escape from his sight; he keeps them within his heart. For they are life to Michael and healing to his flesh.

Proverbs 4:20-22

Healing

He was pierced for Michael's transgressions; He was crushed for his iniquities; upon Him was the chastisement that brought Michael peace, and with His wounds he is healed.

Isaiah 53:5

Then Your light will break forth like the dawn, and Michael's healing will quickly appear; then Your righteousness will go before Michael, and the glory of the Lord will be his rear guard.

Isaiah 58:8

Heal Michael, O Lord, and he shall be healed; save Michael, and he shall be saved, for You are Michael's praise.

Jeremiah 17:14

"Take heart, Michael; your faith has made you well."

Matthew 9:22

Healing

And these signs shall follow Michael, who believes; in Christ's name he shall cast out devils; he shall speak with new tongues; he shall pick up serpents; and if he drinks any deadly thing, it shall not hurt him; he shall lay hands on the sick, and they shall recover.

Mark 16:17-18

And the prayer of faith will save Michael when he is sick, and the Lord will raise him. And if he has committed sins, he will be forgiven.

James 5:15

He Himself bore Michael's sins in His body on the tree, that Michael might die to sin and live to righteousness. By His wounds Michael has been healed.

1 Peter 2:24

Michael, I pray that all may go well with you and that you may be in good health, as it goes well with your soul.

3 John 1:2

Hope

"For I know the plans I have for you Michael," declares the Lord, "plans to prosper you and not to harm you, to give you a future and a hope. Then Michael will call upon me and come and pray to me, and I will hear him. Michael will seek me and find me, when Michael seeks me with all of his heart.

Jeremiah 29:11-13

Michael hopes in the Lord and the Lord renews his strength. Michael will soar on wings like an eagle. Michael will run and not grow weary. Michael will walk and not be faint.

Isaiah 40:31

Michael knows that in all things God works together for the good of those who love Him, and have been called according to His purpose.

Romans 8:28

Hope

May the God of hope fill Michael with all joy and peace in believing, so that by the power of the Holy Spirit Michael may abound in hope.

Romans 15:13

Michael is joyful in hope, patient in affliction, faithful in prayer.

Romans 12:12

Michael rejoices in his sufferings, knowing that suffering produces endurance, and endurance produces character, and character produces hope, and hope does not put Michael to shame, because God's love has been poured into his heart through the Holy Spirit who has been given to him.

Romans 5:3-5

Humility

Michael does not think of himself more highly than he ought, but rather he thinks of himself with sober judgment, in accordance with the faith God has distributed to him.

Romans 12:3

Michael does nothing out of selfish ambition or vain conceit, but in humility he doesn't consider himself better than others. Michael does not only look out for his own interests, but also the interests of others. Michael has this mindset which was also in Christ Jesus.

Philippians 2:3-5

Michael humbles himself before the Lord, and the Lord will lift Michael up.

James 4:10

Michael humbles himself under God's mighty hand, that He may lift him up in due time.

1 Peter 5:6

Identity

Before God formed Michael in the womb He knew him; before Michael was born He set him apart.

Jeremiah 1:5

Michael is united with the Lord and is one with Him in spirit.

1 Corinthians 6:17

Michael has been crucified with Christ. Michael no longer lives, but Christ lives in him. The life Michael lives in the flesh he lives by faith in the Son of God, who loved him and gave himself for him.

Galatians 2:20

Michael is God's workmanship, created in Christ Jesus to do good works, which God created in advance for Michael to do.

Ephesians 2:10

Identity

God, as one of Your chosen people, holy and dearly loved, help Michael to clothe himself with compassion, kindness, humility, gentleness and patience.

Colossians 3:12

The Spirit of the Lord is upon Michael because He has anointed Michael to preach the good news to the poor. He has sent Michael to bind up the brokenhearted, to proclaim freedom for the captives and release from darkness for the prisoners, to proclaim the year of the Lord's favor and the day of vengeance of our God. Michael comforts those who mourn, and provides for those who grieve in Zion. Michael bestows on them a crown of beauty instead of ashes, the oil of gladness instead of mourning and a garment of praise instead of the spirit of despair.

Isaiah 61:1-3

Joy

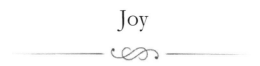

Michael does not grieve, for the joy of the Lord is Michael's strength.

Nehemiah 8:10

The Lord is Michael's strength and shield; Michael's heart trusts in him, and he helps Michael. Michael's heart leaps for joy, and with a song Michael praises him.

Psalm 28:7

Though Michael has not seen Him, he loves Him; and even though Michael does not see Him now, he believes in Him and is filled with an inexpressible and glorious joy, for Michael is receiving the end result of his faith, the salvation of his soul.

1 Peter 1:8-9

Love

Michael loves the Lord with all of his heart, and with all of his soul, and with all of his strength.

Deuteronomy 6:5

Michael's love prospers; he is forgiving. Michael never dwells on a fault because it can separate close friends.

Proverbs 17:9

May Michael have power, together with all of the Lord's holy people, to grasp how wide and long and high and deep is the love of Christ.

Ephesians 3:18

And this is my prayer: that Michael's love may abound more and more in knowledge and depth of insight, so that Michael may be able to discern what is best and may be pure and blameless for the day of Christ.

Philippians 1:9-10

Obedience

As Michael listens to these commands of the Lord, and is careful to obey them, the Lord will make Michael the head and not the tail, and Michael will always be at the top and never at the bottom.

Deuteronomy 28:13

Michael walks in obedience to all that the Lord his God has commanded him, so that he may live and prosper and prolong his days in the land that he will possess.

Deuteronomy 5:33

Michael seeks You with all his heart; Michael will not stray from Your commands; Michael has hidden Your word in his heart that he may not sin against You.

Psalm 119:10-11

Obedience

Michael does not walk in the counsel of the ungodly or stand in the path of sinners or sit in the seat of scoffers. But Michael delights himself in the law of the Lord and Michael meditates on His law day and night. Michael is like a tree planted by the rivers of water, which yields its fruit in season and whose leaf will not wither, and whatever he does he prospers.

Psalm 1:1-3

Michael obeys his parents in the Lord. Michael honors his father and mother so that it may go well with him and that Michael may enjoy long life on earth.

Ephesians 6:1-3

Michael is a doer of the word, not a hearer only, deceiving himself.

James 1:22

Peace

Great peace has Michael, who loves your law, and nothing can make him stumble.

Psalm 119:165

Michael is kept in perfect peace. Michael's mind is steadfast, because he trusts in You.

Isaiah 26:3

Great is the peace of Michael, for he is taught by the Lord.

Isaiah 54:13

Michael will go out in joy and be led forth in peace; the mountains and hills will burst into song before him, and all the trees of the field will clap their hands.

Isaiah 55:12

Peace

Jesus left Michael with a gift: peace of mind and heart. And the peace Jesus gave isn't like the peace the world gives. So Michael is not troubled or afraid.

John 14:27

Michael is not anxious about anything, but in everything by prayer and supplication with thanksgiving he lets his requests be made known to God. And the peace of God, which surpasses all understanding, guards Michael's heart and mind in Christ Jesus.

Philippians 4:6-7

Perseverance

Michael will not be overcome by evil circumstances. Michael will be long remembered. Michael does not fear bad news; he confidently trusts the Lord to care for him.

Psalm 112:6-7

Michael rejoices in his sufferings, because he knows that suffering produces perseverance, perseverance produces character, and character hope, and hope does not disappoint us.

Romans 5:3-4

Michael knows that in all things God works together for the good of those who love Him, and have been called according to His purpose.

Romans 8:28

Perseverance

Forgetting what is behind, and straining toward what is ahead, Michael presses on towards the goal to win the prize for which God has called him heavenward in Christ Jesus.

Philippians 3:13-14

Michael rejoices always, prays continually, and gives thanks in all circumstances; for this is God's will for Michael in Christ Jesus.

1 Thessalonians 5:16-18

Michael never tires of doing what is good.

2 Thessalonians 3:13

Michael does not throw away this confident trust in the Lord. Michael is richly rewarded. Michael patiently endures, so that he will continue to do God's will. Then Michael will receive all that he has been promised.

Hebrews 10:35-36

Perseverance

Perseverance is finishing its work in Michael. Michael is mature and complete in Christ, not lacking anything. Michael asks God for wisdom and God gives Michael wisdom generously without finding fault.

James 1:4-5

Michael counts it all joy, my brothers, when he meets trials of various kinds, for he knows that the testing of his faith produces steadfastness. Michael lets steadfastness have its full effect, so that he may be perfect and complete, lacking in nothing.

James 1:2-4

In this Michael greatly rejoices, though now for a while he may have to suffer grief and all kinds of trials. These have come so that his faith—of greater worth than gold, which perishes even though refined by fire—may result in praise, glory and honor when Jesus Christ is revealed.

Peter 1:6-7

Prayer

Michael prayed for his child, and the Lord has granted him what he asked of Him.

1 Samuel 1:27

Michael cries out, and the Lord hears, and delivers him out of his troubles.

Psalm 34:17

Michael calls upon God, and the Lord saves him. Evening, morning, and at noon, Michael will pray and cry aloud, and God hears his voice. God has redeemed Michael's soul in peace from the battle waged against him.

Psalm 55:16-18

And this is the confidence that Michael has toward Him, that if he asks anything according to His will He hears him.

1 John 5:14

Prayer

The Spirit helps Michael in weakness; for although Michael may not know how he should pray, the Spirit Himself intercedes for Michael with groanings too deep for words; and he who searches our hearts knows what the mind of the Spirit is, because He intercedes for Michael according to the will of God.

Romans 8:26-27

Michael rejoices always, prays without ceasing, gives thanks in all circumstances; for this is the will of God in Christ Jesus for him.

1 Thessalonians 5:16-18

With confidence Michael draws near to the throne of grace, that he may receive mercy and find grace to help him in time of need.

Hebrews 4:16

Michael casts all his cares on God because He cares for Michael.

1 Peter 5:7

Promise

Michael has been trained up in the way he should go; and when he is old, he will not depart from it.

Proverbs 22:6

"And I will give Michael a new heart, and a new spirit I will put within him. And I will remove the heart of stone from Michael's flesh and give him a heart of flesh. And I will put my spirit within Michael, and cause him to walk in my statutes and he will be careful to obey my rules."

Ezekiel 36:26-27

He who began a good work in Michael will be faithful to complete it.

Philippians 1:6

As Michael draws near to God, God draws near to Michael.

James 4:8

Provision

The Lord is Michael's shepherd; Michael lacks nothing.

Psalm 23:1

The lions may grow weak and hungry, but Michael seeks the Lord and lacks no good thing.

Psalm 34:10

For the Lord God is Michael's sun and shield; the Lord bestows favor and honor on Michael; no good thing does He withhold from Michael whose walk is blameless.

Psalm 84:11

The Lord will guide Michael always; He will satisfy Michael's needs in a sun-scorched land and will strengthen Michael's frame. Michael will be like a well-watered garden, like a spring whose waters never fail.

Isaiah 58:11

Provision

And God is able to make all grace abound to Michael, so that in all things at all times, Michael has all that he needs; Michael will abound in every good work.

2 Corinthians 9:8

And my God will meet all of Michael's needs according to the riches of His glory, Christ Jesus.

Philippians 4:19

His divine power has given Michael everything he needs for life and godliness through his knowledge of Him who called Michael by His own glory and goodness.

2 Peter 1:3

Purity

Create in Michael a clean heart, O God, and renew a right spirit within him.

Psalm 51:10

Blessed is Michael, who is pure in heart, for he will see God.

Matthew 5:8

If Michael confesses his sins, He is faithful and righteous to forgive his sins, and to cleanse Michael from all unrighteousness.

1 John 1:9

Purity

Grace and peace be multiplied unto Michael through the knowledge of God, and of Jesus our Lord. His divine power has granted to Michael all things that pertain to life and godliness, through the knowledge of Him who called Michael to his glory and excellence, by which he has granted to Michael his precious and very great promises, so that through them Michael may become a partaker of the divine nature, having escaped from the corruption that is in the world because of sinful desire.

2 Peter 1:1-4

Redemption

Michael calls upon God, and the Lord saves him. Evening, morning, and at noon, Michael will pray and cry aloud, and God hears his voice. God has redeemed Michael's soul in peace from the battle waged against him.

Psalm 55:16-18

Do not gloat over Michael, enemy! Though Michael has fallen, he will rise; though Michael sits in darkness, the Lord will be his light. Because he has sinned against Him, he will bear the consequences, until He pleads Michael's case and establishes his right. He will bring Michael into the light and Michael will see His righteousness.

Micah 7:8-9

Michael has been crucified with Christ. Michael no longer lives, but Christ lives in him. The life Michael now lives in the body, he lives by faith in the Son of God, who loved him and gave Himself for him.

Galatians 2:20

Revelation

Do not gloat over Michael, enemy! Though Michael has fallen, he will rise; though Michael sits in darkness, the Lord will be his light. Because he has sinned against Him, he will bear the consequences, until He pleads Michael's case and establishes his right. He will bring Michael into the light and Michael will see His righteousness.

Micah 7:8-9

What Michael has received is not the spirit of the world, but the Spirit who is from God, so that he may understand what God has freely given him.

1 Corinthians 2:12

Michael has the mind of Christ and the wisdom of God is formed within him.

1 Corinthians 2:16

Revelation

God, bring to light and remove any darkness in Michael's heart. He will expose any wrong motives to him.

1 Corinthians 4:5

Whenever Michael turns to the Lord, the veil is taken away.

2 Corinthians 3:16

May the Lord Jesus Christ give Michael the Spirit of wisdom and of revelation in the knowledge of Him, having the eyes of his heart enlightened, that Michael may know what is the hope to which He has called him, what are the riches of his glorious inheritance in the saints, and what is the immeasurable greatness of His power toward us who believe, according to the working of His great might.

Ephesians 1:17-19

Righteousness

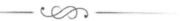

The Lord dealt with Michael according to his righteousness; according to the cleanness of his hands He rewarded him.

2 Samuel 22:21

Michael clothes himself with the Lord Jesus Christ, and does not think about how to gratify the desires of the flesh.

Romans 13:14

He who supplies seed to the sower and bread for food will supply and multiply Michael's seed for sowing and increase the harvest of his righteousness.

2 Corinthians 9:10

Michael is filled with the fruit of righteousness that comes through Jesus Christ, to the glory and praise of God.

Philippians 1:11

Righteousness

Michael flees the evil desires of his youth and pursues righteousness, faith, love, and peace, along with those who call on the Lord out of a pure heart.

2 Timothy 2:22

Safety & Protection

God is Michael's rock, in whom he takes refuge, his shield and the horn of his salvation. He is Michael's stronghold, his refuge and his savior—from violent people Michael is saved. He calls to the Lord, who is worthy of praise, and Michael is saved from his enemies.

2 Samuel 22:3-4

Michael is safe and hidden in the Lord's shadow away from danger.

Psalm 91:1

Do not withhold Your mercy from Michael, O Lord; may Your love and Your truth always protect him.

Psalm 40:11

The Lord's angels keep charge over Michael to guard him in all his ways.

Psalm 91:11

Safety & Protection

Michael's integrity and uprightness protect him, because Michael's hope, Lord, is in You.

Psalm 25:21

Michael has made the Most High his dwelling place. No harm will befall Michael; no disaster will come near his tent. For He will give His angels charge over Michael to guard him in all of his ways. They will carry him so that Michael does not dash his foot against a stone. They will tread upon the lion and the cobra; they will trample them underfoot. Because Michael loves You, You will deliver him. You will set Michael on high. Michael will call upon You and You will answer him. You will be with Michael in trouble. You will deliver Michael and honor him with a long life. You will satisfy Michael and show him Your salvation.

Psalm 91:9-16

Safety & Protection

When Michael lies down, he will not be afraid; when Michael lies down, his sleep will be sweet. Michael has no fear of sudden disaster or of the ruin that overtakes the wicked, for the Lord is at his side and will keep his foot from being snared.

Proverbs 3:24-26

Michael is taught by the Lord and great will be Michael's peace, his health, safety, protection, and prosperity. In righteousness Michael will be established. Tyranny will be far from Michael; Michael will have nothing to fear. Terror will be far removed; it will not come near Michael. No weapon forged against Michael will prosper.

Isaiah 54:13-14, 17

Michael is afflicted in every way, but not crushed; perplexed, but not driven to despair; persecuted, but not forsaken; struck down, but not destroyed.

2 Corinthians 4:8-9

Salvation

Michael calls upon God, and the Lord saves him. Evening, morning, and at noon, Michael will pray and cry aloud, and God hears his voice. God has redeemed Michael's soul in peace from the battle waged against him.

Psalm 55:16-18

I am convinced that neither death nor life, neither angels nor demons, neither the present nor the future, nor any powers, neither height nor depth, nor anything else in all creation, will be able to separate Michael from the love of God that is in Christ Jesus our Lord.

Romans 8:38-39

Michael confesses with his mouth that Jesus is Lord and Michael believes in his heart that You have raised Christ from the dead. Michael calls on Your name, Lord! Michael is saved as one of Your children.

Romans 10:9-13

Salvation

Michael finds his salvation in repentance and rest. Michael's strength is in quietness and trust.

Isaiah 30:15

Michael is a new creation in Christ Jesus.

2 Corinthians 5:17

Praise be to the God and Father of our Lord Jesus Christ! In His great mercy He has given Michael new birth into a living hope through the resurrection of Jesus Christ from the dead, and into an inheritance that can never perish, spoil, or fade. This inheritance is kept in heaven for Michael, who through faith is shielded by God's power until the coming of the salvation that is ready to be revealed in the last time.

1 Peter 1:3-4

Seeking God

Michael will seek the Lord his God and he will find Him, if he searches after Him with all his heart and with all his soul.

Deuteronomy 4:29

Deal bountifully with Michael, that he may live and keep Your word. Open Michael's eyes that he may behold wondrous things out of the word.

Psalm 119:17-18

O God, You are Michael's God, earnestly he seeks You; Michael's soul thirsts for You, his body longs for You, in a dry and weary land where there is no water. Michael has seen You in the sanctuary and beheld Your power and Your glory. Because Your love is better than life, Michael's lips will glorify You.

Psalm 63:1-3

Seeking God

"I Love Michael who loves me, and as Michael seeks me so he will find me."

Proverbs 8:17

"Michael will call upon me and come and pray to me, and I will hear him. Michael will seek me and find me, when he seeks me with all his heart. I will be found by Michael," declares the Lord.

Jeremiah 29:12-14

The Lord is good to Michael whose hope is in Him, to Michael who seeks Him.

Lamentations 3:25

Michael has the mind of Christ and the wisdom of God is formed within him.

1 Corinthians 2:16

Seeking God

Forgetting what is behind, and straining toward what is ahead, Michael presses on towards the goal to win the prize for which God has called him heavenward in Christ Jesus.

Philippians 3:13-14

Michael draws near to God, and He draws near to him.

James 4:8

Though Michael has not seen Him, he loves Him; and even though Michael does not see Him now, he believes in Him and is filled with an inexpressible and glorious joy, for Michael is receiving the end result of his faith, the salvation of his soul.

1 Peter 1:8-9

Spiritual Growth

He who supplies seed to the sower and bread for food will supply and multiply Michael's seed for sowing and increase the harvest of his righteousness.

2 Corinthians 9:10

Michael, speaking the truth in love, grows up in every way into Him who is the head, into Christ.

Ephesians 4:15

Michael walks in a manner worthy of the Lord, fully pleasing Him, bearing fruit in every good work and growing in the knowledge of God. Michael is strengthened with all power according to His glorious might so that he has great endurance and patience.

Colossians 1:10-11

Michael leaves the elementary doctrine of Christ and goes on to maturity, not laying again the foundation of repentance from dead works and of faith in God.

Hebrews 6:1

Spiritual Growth

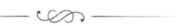

Michael is growing in the grace and knowledge of our Lord and savior Jesus Christ. To Him be glory both now and forever! Amen.

2 Peter 3:18

Spiritual Warfare

Michael is strong in the Lord and in his mighty power. Michael puts on the full armor of God, so that he can take his stand against the devil's schemes. For Michael's struggles are not against flesh and blood, but against the rulers, against the authorities, against the powers of this dark world and against the spiritual forces of evil in the heavenly realms. Therefore, Michael puts on the full armor of God, so that when the day of evil comes, Michael will stand his ground. Michael stands firm with the belt of truth buckled around his waist, with the breastplate of righteousness in place, and with his feet fitted with the readiness that comes from the gospel of peace. In addition to all this, Michael takes up the shield of faith, with which he can extinguish all the flaming arrows of the evil one. Michael takes the helmet of salvation and the sword of the Spirit, which is the word of God.

Ephesians 6:10-17

Spiritual Warfare

Michael calls upon God, and the Lord saves him. Evening, morning, and at noon, Michael will pray and cry aloud, and God hears his voice. God has redeemed Michael's soul in peace from the battle waged against him.

Psalm 55:16-18

Michael has authority to trample on snakes and scorpions and to overcome all the power of the enemy; nothing will harm Michael.

Luke 10:19

In all things Michael is more than a conqueror through Him who loved us. For I am convinced that neither death nor life, neither angels nor demons, neither the present nor future, nor any powers, neither height nor depth, nor anything else in all creation, will be able to separate Michael from the love of God that is in Christ Jesus our Lord.

Romans 8:37-39

Spiritual Warfare

Michael is not overcome by evil, but Michael overcomes evil with good.

Romans 12:21

No temptation has overtaken Michael except what is common to mankind. And God is faithful; He will not let Michael be tempted beyond what he can bear. But when Michael is tempted, He will also provide a way out so that he can endure it.

1 Corinthians 10:13

Michael demolishes arguments and every pretension that sets itself up against the knowledge of God, and Michael takes captive every thought and makes it obedient to Christ.

2 Corinthians 10:5

Spiritual Warfare

Michael is delivered from the evils of this present world, for it is the will of God.

Galatians 1:4

Michael is an overcomer and Michael overcomes by the blood of the Lamb and the word of his testimony.

Revelation 12:11

Strength

It is God who arms Michael with strength and makes his way perfect. God makes Michael's feet like the feet of a deer; He enables Michael to stand on the heights.

2 Samuel 22:33-34

The joy of the Lord is Michael's strength. The Lord is the strength of Michael's life.

Nehemiah 8:10

Create in Michael a pure heart, O God, and renew a steadfast spirit within him. Restore to Michael the joy of Your salvation and grant him a willing spirit, to sustain him.

Psalm 51:10,12

Strength

Michael does not walk in the counsel of the ungodly or stand in the path of sinners or sit in the seat of scoffers. But Michael delights himself in the law of the Lord and Michael meditates on His law day and night. Michael is like a tree planted by the rivers of water, which yields its fruit in season and whose leaf will not wither, and whatever he does he prospers.

Psalm 1:1-3

Michael will never be shaken; Michael will be remembered forever. Michael will not fear bad news; his heart is steadfast, trusting in the Lord. Michael's heart is upheld, he will not fear.

Psalm 112:6-8

The Lord makes firm the steps of Michael who delights in him; though Michael stumbles, he will not fall, for the Lord upholds him with His hand.

Psalm 37:23-24

Strength

Michael finds his salvation in repentance and rest. Michael's strength is in quietness and trust.

Isaiah 30:15

Michael hopes in the Lord and the Lord renews his strength. Michael will soar on wings like an eagle. Michael will run and not grow weary. Michael will walk and not be faint.

Isaiah 40:31

Greater is He who is in Michael, than he who is in the world.

1 John 4:4

Michael receives the gift of the Holy Spirit. Michael receives power when the Holy Spirit comes upon him.

Acts 1:8

Michael can do all things through Christ who strengthens him.

Philippians 4:13

Strength

Michael walks in a manner worthy of the Lord, fully pleasing Him, bearing fruit in every good work and growing in the knowledge of God. Michael is strengthened with all power according to His glorious might so that he has great endurance and patience.

Colossians 1:10-11

Just as Michael received Christ Jesus as Lord, he continues to live in Him. Michael is rooted and built up in Him, strengthened in faith as he was taught, and overflowing with thankfulness.

Colossians 2:6-7

The Lord is faithful, and He will strengthen Michael and protect him from the evil one.

2 Thessalonians 3:3

Transformation

Michael delights himself in the Lord and the Lord gives Michael the desires of his heart.

Psalm 37:4

Michael is not conformed to the pattern of this world but he is transformed by the renewing of his mind. Michael's mind is renewed by the word of God.

Romans 12:22

Michael is a new creation in Christ Jesus.

2 Corinthians 5:17

Michael does not lose heart. Though outwardly he is wasting away, yet inwardly Michael is being renewed day by day, for Michael's light and momentary troubles are achieving for him an eternal glory that far outweighs them all. So Michael fixes his eyes not on what is seen, but what is unseen, since what is seen is temporary, but what is unseen is eternal.

2 Corinthians 4:16-18

Transformation

Michael has been crucified with Christ and he no longer lives, but Christ lives in him. The life Michael now lives in the body, he lives by faith in the Son of God, who loved Michael and gave Himself for him.

Galatians 2:20

He who began a good work in Michael will be faithful to complete it.

Philippians 1:6

May God Himself, the God of peace, sanctify Michael through and through. May Michael's whole spirit, soul, and body be kept blameless at the coming of our Lord Jesus Christ.

1 Thessalonians 5:23

Trials

Indeed, Michael felt that he had received the sentence of death. But that was to make him rely not on himself but on God who raises the dead.

2 Corinthians 1:9

And the God of all grace, who called Michael to His eternal glory in Christ, after Michael has suffered a little while, will Himself restore him and make him strong, firm and steadfast.

1 Peter 5:10

In all this Michael greatly rejoices, though now for a little while he may have had to suffer grief in all kinds of trials. These have come so that the proven genuineness of Michael's faith—of greater worth than gold, which perishes even though refined by fire—may result in praise, glory, and honor when Jesus Christ is revealed.

1 Peter 1:6-7

Trust

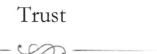

Some trust in chariots and some in horses, but Michael trusts in the name of the Lord our God.

Psalm 20:7

Michael trusts in the Lord with all his heart, and does not lean on his own understanding. In all Michael's ways he acknowledges Him, and He will direct his path.

Proverbs 3:5-6

Michael does not throw away his confident trust in the Lord. Michael is richly rewarded. Michael has patient endurance so that he continues to do God's will. Then Michael will receive all that he has been promised.

Hebrews 10:35-36

Wisdom

The Spirit of the Lord will rest on Michael—the Spirit of wisdom and of understanding, the Spirit of counsel and of might, the Spirit of the knowledge and fear of the Lord.

Isaiah 11:2

I keep asking that the God of our Lord Jesus Christ, the glorious Father, may give Michael the Spirit of wisdom and revelation, so that he may know him better. I pray that the eyes of Michael's heart may be enlightened in order that he may know the hope to which He has called him, the riches of his glorious inheritance in His holy people, and His incomparably great power for us who believe.

Ephesians 1:17-19

And this is my prayer: that Michael's love may abound more and more in knowledge and depth of insight so that Michael may be able to discern what is best and may be pure and blameless until the day of Christ. May Michael be filled with the fruit of righteousness that comes through Jesus Christ to the glory and praise of God.

Philippians 1:9-11

Wisdom

Michael is filled with the knowledge of the Lord's will and all wisdom and spiritual understanding.

Colossians 1:19

When Michael lacks wisdom, he asks God who gives generously to all without finding fault, and it will be given to him.

James 1:5

Worship

Michael trusts in Your unfailing love; his heart rejoices in Your salvation. Michael sings to the Lord, for He has been good to him.

Psalm 13:5-6

In view of God's mercy, Michael offers his body as a living sacrifice, holy and pleasing to God—this is his spiritual act of worship.

Romans 12:1

Michael is grateful for receiving a kingdom that cannot be shaken, and he offers to God acceptable worship, with reverence and awe, for our God is a consuming fire.

Hebrews 12:28-29

Michael fears God and gives Him glory, because the hour of his judgment has come. Michael worships Him who made the heavens, the earth, the sea and the springs of water.

Revelation 14:7

AUTHOR'S NOTE

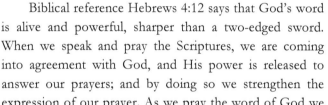

Biblical reference Hebrews 4:12 says that God's word is alive and powerful, sharper than a two-edged sword. When we speak and pray the Scriptures, we are coming into agreement with God, and His power is released to answer our prayers; and by doing so we strengthen the expression of our prayer. As we pray the word of God we will learn who He is, and who He has made us to be. When we are living in the fullness of our true identity in Christ, we will then experience God and all He has intended for us.

TESTIMONY

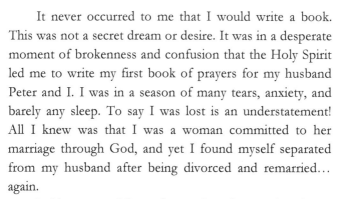

It never occurred to me that I would write a book. This was not a secret dream or desire. It was in a desperate moment of brokenness and confusion that the Holy Spirit led me to write my first book of prayers for my husband Peter and I. I was in a season of many tears, anxiety, and barely any sleep. To say I was lost is an understatement! All I knew was that I was a woman committed to her marriage through God, and yet I found myself separated from my husband after being divorced and remarried... again.

I felt regret, failure, fear, exhaustion, and sadness. Somehow, having been in this situation before didn't help any. In fact it made me feel worse. My prayer life was barely alive because I found myself in such a pathetic state. Sometimes all I could pray was "I trust You, Lord." Being so empty, this statement was all I had to offer. I was so messed up that it felt like I said it every thirty seconds.

I entered into a season in which the Lord told me not to talk to my husband. All of our conversations were leading to more division. The only way God allowed me to contact Peter was by sending him loving or encouraging text messages and scriptures. He also led me to start writing scriptures down and inserting our names into them. Although still broken, my prayers were empowered. I was praying God's will for our lives. I was unleashing the power of the Holy Spirit into my marriage. I wrote these scriptures on little white spiral-bound note cards. This task sustained me through a terrible time, transformed both of our hearts, and I believe it brought my husband and I back together.

I understand that not all trials end in victory. Because Peter and I are human, we will have struggles again. But I will never stop using the gift that God gave me. It changes me continually. And during the time I described above the prayers enabled me to function as a mom in an upside-down world.

I soon realized the power these little books had and started writing them for my children and for the people around me who were going through tough times. The response was unbelievable. I heard things like "This is just what I needed," and many stories of hope and change.

If you are looking to grow in your relationship with God or to overcome a difficult situation, I encourage you to pray this little book and to pray it for those you love. Get ready to be transformed and to be a world changer. Life will never be the same.

ABOUT THE AUTHOR

Michelle Leslie was raised in rural Oregon. She is a pillar of activation within the Body of Christ with a heart to hear God's word and see it lived out as her calling and destiny. Along with her gift for challenging people to be all they were created to be in their life, she is a fun-loving, hard-working, creative friend, daughter, mom, and wife.

As a child, Michelle was dyslexic. Because of her trouble learning to read, she struggled through every subject in school and was doomed to special education classes (which she perceived as "social suicide"). When Michelle came to know the Lord in her early twenties she was desperate for God's word. As she dove into the word of God, her life changed dramatically. Romans 12:2 was in full effect, and Michelle was transformed by the renewing of her mind. The effects of the learning disability that had held Michelle back her whole life were slowly diminishing. Michelle was finally reading and retaining information, growing in confidence, and developing a voice for the message God had given her to share. God's power was being made perfect in her weakness, and through this platform God demonstrated his love and transforming power to those around her.

Michelle has a deep desire for others to experience the transformation and freedom that can only be found in Christ, and she is sharing it with all who will listen through this extraordinary upcoming book, *Activating God's Power*.

Michelle is writing in the hope of meeting the needs of readers in desperation, or those who are seeking spiritual growth in themselves or in their loved ones. Michelle lives in Denver, Colorado with her husband and two daughters.

CONTACT

To order books please see instructions at:
www.MichelleLeslie.net

To contact Michelle Leslie directly:
Michelle@MichelleLeslie.net

Follow Michelle Leslie online:

Facebook.com/MichelleLeslie.net

@MichelleLeslie_

MichelleLeslie_

Made in the USA
San Bernardino, CA
15 January 2017